Pump Carving Stencils

FOR ADVANCED

Over 60 Spooky Stencils for Halloween
Pumpkin Carving Fun PLUS 100+
Rib-Tickling Halloween Jokes!

HOW TO USE

1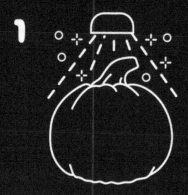

STEP 1: WASH ANY DUST AND DIRT FROM THE PUMPKIN

2

STEP 2: CHOOSE A STENCIL AND CUT IT OUT ALONG THE DOTTED LINE

3

STEP 3: GLUE OR TAPE THE STENCIL ONTO THE PUMPKIN

STEP 4: TRACE THE STENCIL BY POKING HOLES THROUGH THE PAPER AND INTO THE PUMPKIN, USING A FORK OR SHARPENED PENCIL

4

5

STEP 5: REMOVE THE STENCIL AND USE A CRAFT KNIFE TO CAREFULLY CARVE THE PUMPKIN

STEP 6: GUT THE PUMPKIN, CUT THE TOP OFF, AND PLACE A CANDLE OR LED LIGHT INSIDE THE PUMPKIN

6

Why are graveyards so noisy?

Because of all the coffin.

Why did the ghost quit studying?

Because he was too ghoul for school.

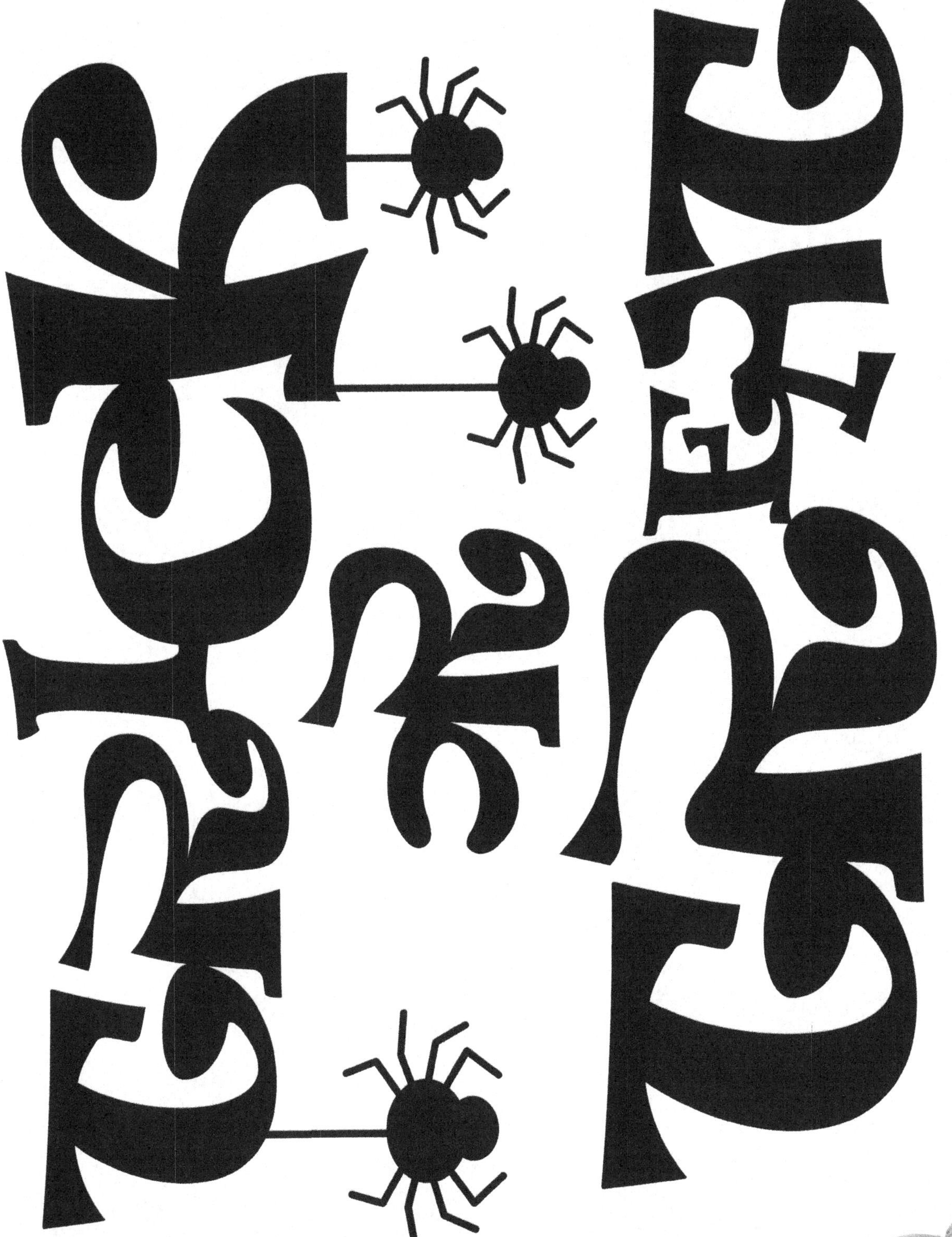
TRICK
or
TREAT
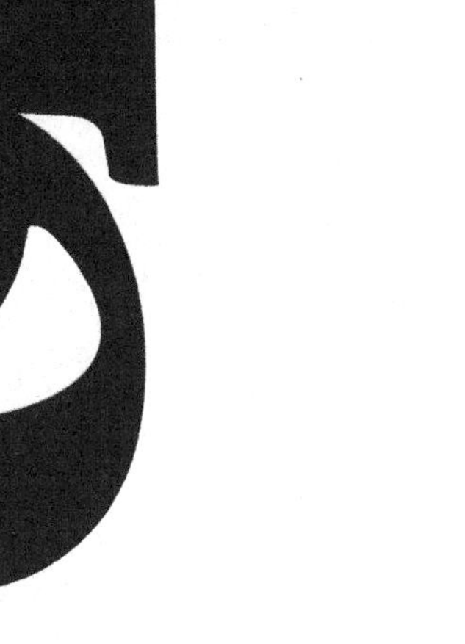
TRICK
or
TREAT

What kind of medicine do witches use on their warts?

I don't know, but it's not working.

What happened to the witch who flew her broom while angry?

She flew off the handle.

Why did the zombie become a mortician?

To put food on the table.

Where did the skeleton keep his money?

In the crypt-o market.

Where do zombies live?

On a dead-end street.

What kind of art do skeletons like?

Skulltures.

Where do ghosts buy their food?

At the ghost-ery store!

What type of plants do well on all Hallow's Eve?

Bam-BOO!

Why can't skeletons play church music?

Because they have no organs.

How do you know if a Zombie likes someone?

They ask for seconds.

Knock   Knock?   Who's
there?   Witch!   Witch
who? Witch one of you
has my candy?

Do   you   know   any
skeleton jokes?

Yes, but you wouldn't
find it very humerus.

What's a Zombie's favorite treat?

You might guess brain food, but it's actually eye candy.

What's a pumpkin's favorite Western?

The Gourd, the Bad, and the Ugly

Knock Knock? Who's there? Ivana! Ivana who? Ivana suck your blood!

Why did the witch take a nap?

She needed to rest a spell.

Why did he jack-o-lantern fail out of school?

Someone scooped his brains out.

Why don't werewolves ever know the time?

Because they're not whenwolves.

I dropped my pumpkin yesterday. Jack-o-lantern? More like crack-o-lantern!

Why couldn't the mummy go to school with the witch?

He couldn't spell.

How do vampires get around on Halloween?

On blood vessels.

Why aren't zombies ever arrested?

They can't be captured alive.

What's a ghost's favorite play?

Romeo and Ghoul-iet.

Knock Knock? Who's there? Phillip! Phillip who? Phillip my bag with candy!

How do you mend a jack-o'-lantern?

With a pumpkin patch.

Why was Cinderella bad at football?

Because she had a pumpkin for a coach.

What do witches get when their shoes are too tight?

Candy corns.

What do you call a movie about Zombies finding true love?

A Zom-com.

Knock Knock? Who's there? Ice cream! Ice Cream who? Ice cream every time I see a ghost!

What do skeletons order at a restaurant?

Spare ribs.

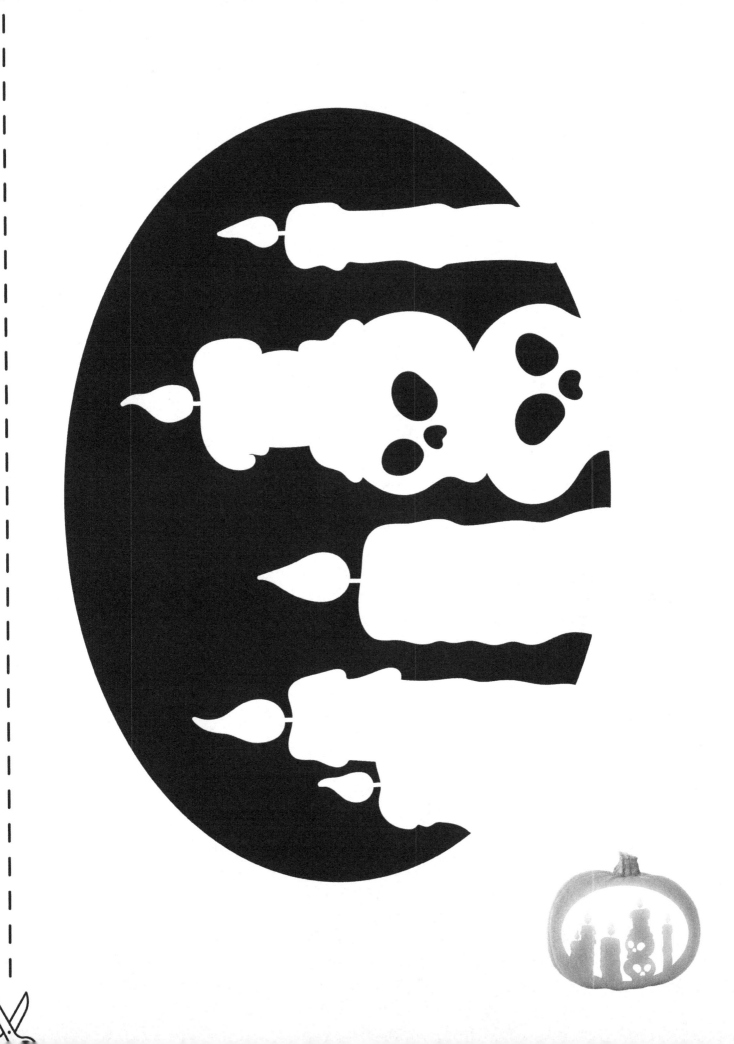

What do you get when
you cross a vampire
and a snowman?

Frostbite.

What's a pumpkin's
favorite genre?

Pulp fiction.

How do you know when a ghost is sad?

He starts boo hooing.

What do you call a mummy covered in chocolate and nuts?

A Pharaoh Roche.

Why do vampires not want to become investment bankers?

They hate stakeholders.

Who helped the little pumpkin cross the road?

The crossing gourd.

How do you get rid of demons?

Exorcise a lot.

What did Dracula say when the witch and the warlock started kissing?

Get a broom!

What's a skeleton's favorite song?

"Bad to the Bone."

Why did Dracula take cold medicine?

Because he was coffin too much.

Knock Knock? Who's there? Figs! Figs who? Figs your doorbell so I can stop knocking!

What was the chicken ghost's name?

Poultrygeist.

What's it like to be kissed by a vampire?

It's a pain in the neck.

What's a witch's favorite makeup?

Ma-scare-a.

What was the witch's favorite subject in school?

Spelling.

How do ghosts send letters?

Through the ghost office.

I would make a skeleton joke, but you wouldn't find it very humerus.

What's a Zombie's favorite cheese?

Zom-brie.

What's a vampire's favorite fruit?

Neck-tarines.

What do you call a witch's garage?

A broom closet.

What do vegetarian zombies eat?

Graaaains!

Why don't mummies take time off?

They're afraid to unwind.

What treat do eye doctors give out on Halloween?

Candy corneas.

Why are vampires bad at art?

They are only able to draw blood.

How do vampires start
their letters?

Tomb it may concern.

Knock   Knock?   Who's
there?   Orange!   Orange
who?   Orange   you   glad
it's Halloween?

What do you get when
you drop a pumpkin?

Squash.

What does a panda
ghost eat?

Bam-BOO!

What do you call a skeleton who goes out in the snow?

A numb-skull.

Where does a mummy go on vacation?

The Dead Sea.

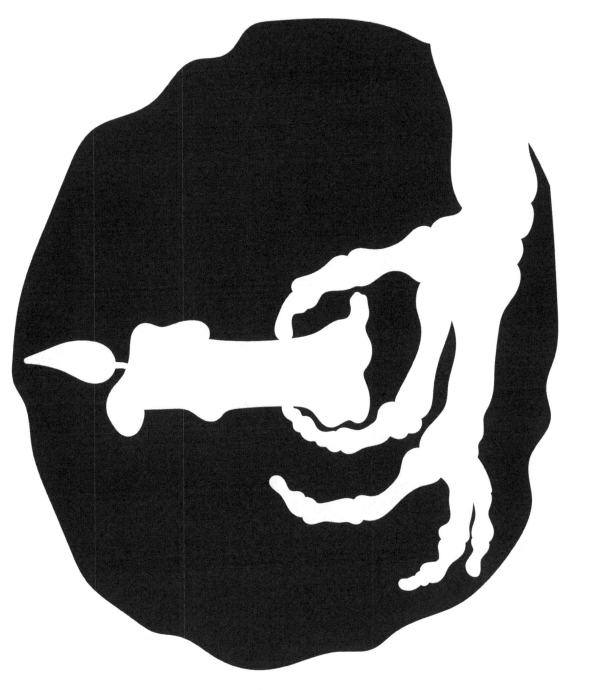

Why do skeletons have low self-esteem?

They have no body to love.

Where does a skeleton go for a fun night?

Anywhere, as long as it's a hip joint.

What do you call Zombies in pajamas?

The sleepwalking dead.

Why didn't the skeleton go to the scary movie?

He didn't have the guts.

Why was the gourd so gossipy?

To give 'em pumpkin to talk about.

Why was the cemetery chosen to be the perfect location to write a movie?

Because it had great plots.

What's the problem with
twin witches?

You never know which
witch is which.

What do you call a
cleaning skeleton?

The grim sweeper.

Why did the vampire
read the newspaper?

He heard it had great
circulation.

What sea do Zombies
swim in?

The dead sea.

Where does a pumpkin preach?

From the pulp-it.

Who won the skeleton beauty contest?

No body.

Why did the skeleton start a fight?

Because he had a bone to pick.

Who helps the little pumpkins cross the road safely?

The crossing gourd.

What does a ghost mom say when she gets in the car?

Fasten your sheet-belts.

How many cannibals does it take to change a lightbulb?

I don't know but you really shouldn't be in the dark with a cannibal.

Why don't zombies eat popcorn with their hands?

They eat their hands separately.

What kind of food would you find on a haunted beach?

A sand-witch!

What brand of shampoo do Zombies use?

Head and Shoulders.

What kind of bread do Zombies like?

Whole brain.

Why did the pumpkin take a detour?

To avoid a seedy part of town.

What kind of music do mummies like listening to on Halloween?

Wrap music.

Why did the pumpkin take a detour?

To avoid a seedy part of town.

What kind of music do mummies like listening to on Halloween?

Wrap music.

How did the witch get around when her broomstick broke?

She witch-hiked.

What is in a ghost's nose?

Boo-gers.

What's a ghost's favorite dessert?

I-Scream!

What is a skeleton's favorite instrument?

A trom-bone.

What's a vampire's favorite ice cream flavor?

Vein-illa.

What room does a ghost not need in a house?

A living room.

What do you call a witch with a rash?

An itchy-witchy.

Why don't I like Dracula?

He's a pain in the neck

Why do ghosts make the best cheerleaders?

They have a lot of spirit!

Where do ghosts go on vacation?

Mali-boo.

Why don't zombies like
pirates?

They're too salty.

What kind of horse do
ghosts ride?

A night-mare

Why does a witch ride a broomstick?

So she can make a clean getaway.

What does the vampire's Valentine say?

You're just my blood type.

What is a Zombie
sleepover called?

Mass grave.

What did the pumpkin
say to its carver?

Cut it out!

What's a vampire's favorite fruit?

Neck-tarines.

What's a Zombie's favorite weather?

Cloudy, with a chance of brain.

How can you tell when a vampire has been in a bakery?

All the jelly has been sucked out of the jelly doughnuts.

What's it called when a vampire has trouble with his house?

A grave problem.

What does a carved pumpkin celebrate?

Hollow-een.

What do you call Ryan Gosling in a mummy costume?

Ryan Gauzeling

Knock Knock? Who's there? Iguana. Iguana who? Iguana eat all your candy.

Knock Knock? Who's there? Boo! Boo who? Don't cry, it's only Halloween.

How do gourds grow big and strong?

Pumpkin iron.

Why don't mummies have friends?

Because they're too wrapped up in themselves.

R.I.P.

Why did the headless horseman go into business?

He wanted to get ahead in life.

How does a witch style her hair?

With scare spray.

Why was the jack-o'-lantern scared?

Because it had no guts.

What do dentists hand out at Halloween?

Candy.

Knock Knock? Who's there? Eddie! Eddie who? Eddie body home? It's Halloween!

Know why skeletons are so calm?

Because nothing gets under their skin.

What do you call two witches who live together?

Broom-mates!

What's the best thing to put into a pumpkin pie?

Your teeth.

Who's the scariest body
builder of all time?

Dr. Frankenstein.

How do mummies tell
their future?

They read their horror-
scope.

Made in the USA
Middletown, DE
16 October 2023